INSIDEAARD

INSIDEAARD

First published in 2000 by
ScreenPress Books
8 Queen Square
Southwold
Suffolk
IP18 6EQ

Compiled by James Oliver
Designed by Sarah Theodosiou
Printed by Hoonte Boscht & Keuning, Netherlands

CIP record for this book is available from the British Library

ISBN 1 091680 52 5

For information on forthcoming film books from ScreenPress books please
contact the publishers at the address above or:
fax: 01502 725422
email: mail@screenpress.co.uk
or visit our web site at www.screenpress.co.uk

Contents

Creature Comforts, Bushbaby

Foreword by Peter Lord/David Sproxton

We began animating as a hobby as teenagers, almost thirty years ago, and although animation now has become a career, it has never stopped being a hobby. Other boys of our age were spending their leisure time building model aircraft or recording train numbers or sitting on the river bank awaiting the appearance of fish. But Fate led us to animation.

Together we picked the name Aardman, based on one of our earliest characters. We never dreamed that it would hang around for so long. Now, all these years later the name no longer stands for a couple of enthusiastic schoolboy film-makers; instead we are a company running our own film studio. But the impulse that drives us is still the same. We want to make films, though the reasons why have evolved over the years. Initially, it was simple: two young men making short films to amuse themselves for the pleasure of creation, for the pleasure of communication, to show off, to do something a little different, to get a laugh, to affect people we had never met. Later, as Aardman got bigger and more established, we discovered we were not just individuals working on our own but part of a much wider community of film-makers in Britain and abroad. The big pleasure for me at this stage in Aardman's evolution is the feeling of being among dozens of creative people, generating ideas, discussing them, interacting, being influenced and affected by each other.

The fact that the Aardman studios are such an exciting place today is the best testimony to our ongoing vision.

History of Aardman

Early Days

It all started with two school friends messing about with a camera. David Sproxton's father owned a 16mm Bolex cine camera. One day they decided to try their hand at animation. By the simple method of pointing their camera at a black-board and patiently drawing and erasing a chalk figure, they created their very first animation. It was a modest start – a world away from the technical sophistication of *Chicken Run* – but the seeds had been sown. When the film returned from the lab and they saw the fruits of their labours, Sproxton and Lord were hooked.

Wat' s Pig

Inspired by the films of Ray Harryhausen, the duo began to experiment with stop-motion animation, creating their figures from Plasticine (known in America as modelling clay) and patiently animating them. David Sproxton says, 'Clay animation must be one of the simplest forms of animation to achieve, as you don't even need to be able to draw! With a simple camera set up and a pack of Harbutt's best, you're on your way.'

The two budding animators continued to hone their skills on the kitchen table. David Sproxton's father, Vernon, was a producer for the BBC and managed to show a demonstration reel of their work to the producer of *Vision On*, a programme aimed at deaf viewers which was at the time the only show-case for animation on British television. Suitably impressed, the producer commissioned them to do work for the pro-gramme. Neither Sproxton nor Lord is a formally trained ani-mator. Instead, over this period, they refined their animation and film-making skills, learning from both their successes and their mistakes until they had achieved a thorough grounding in their chosen field.

All of a sudden they were a company and they needed a name, so they could bank their earnings (a colossal £25). They called their fledgling organization after one of their char-acters, a Superman parody (complete with underpants worn outside his trousers) called Aardman. Ironically, despite being famed for their stop-motion work, the original Aardman charac-ter was a more traditional cel animation. But the unusual name gave their company a distinctive identity and had the added bonus of ensuring that they were always first in the phone book.

A Very Brief History of Stop Motion

Stop-motion animation, the technique that Aardman were to specialize in, has a long history. The great pioneer of imaginative cinema Georges Méliès began experimenting with animation in

Owzat

the 1890s by physically drawing on the film. Others refined this technique and the first cel animations were produced in the first decade of the twentieth century. In 1915, a former sculptor called Willis O'Brien decided to try animation using models. The technique led to his first film, *The Dinosaur and the Missing Link,* and a contract with the Edison Company. In 1922, O'Brien began work on a film version of Arthur Conan Doyle's *The Lost World*, which was eventually completed in 1925. O'Brien's effects were so convincing that when Conan Doyle showed them to Harry Houdini and claimed they were real dinosaurs, the legendary escapologist believed him. O'Brien's next major project was the greatest monster movie of them all, *King Kong.*

O'Brien's dinosaurs were enough to convince Ray Harryhausen that he should take up animation. Like Sproxton and Lord, he was self-taught, and eventually he managed to persuade his idol to offer him a job. He assisted O'Brien on another monkey movie (the original *Mighty Joe Young*) before teaming up with producer Charles H. Schneer to make fantasy films. Their most famous film, *Jason and the Argonauts*, shows some of Harryhausen's best work, with the heroic Jason battling against skeletons born from the teeth of the hydra. Harryhausen's unique hands-on approach was very popular with audiences, but less so with financiers, who had to wait literally years for the hand-crafted effects to be finished.

Animation elsewhere was looked on as an art form in its own right, not simply as a means of producing special effects, and flourished particularly in the communist states. An excellent example of this more artistic school of animation is provided by the work of Czechoslovakian Jan Svankmajer, who blends his experience of puppetry with animation and live action to create surreal, unnerving pieces. After the Soviet crackdown of 1968, many Czech animators fled their country

Creature Comforts

and came to Britain, where they produced work for *Vision On*, the same programme that gave Aardman their first commission. More recently, the American Brothers Quay have produced many disturbing and influential animations, influenced by Svankmajer's work (they also contributed to Aardman's video for Peter Gabriel's 'Sledgehammer').

In the UK, when Sproxton and Lord set up their company, animation was seen primarily as a means of providing entertainment for children. Serge Danot's *Magic Roundabout* was revoiced for the children's market (in spite of its cult appeal to adults) and the BBC broadcast series like *Trumpton* and *Camberwick Green*, which consisted of very basic stop motion. Consequently, Aardman set aside their desire to make more sophisticated animations and concentrated on work for *Vision On*.

Morph

Aardman soon began to contribute more to *Vision On*. Their work was very popular with the producers of the programme, who invited them to become further involved in the show. To this end, they came up with a character called Morph. Morph was a small, brown, Plasticine man who acted as foil to the show's presenter, Tony Hart. As the name suggests, Morph had a habit of 'morphing' into other objects. He specialized in irritating Tony, who usually retaliated by squashing Morph. These animations were massively successful and distinguished the programme from many others. Although *Vision On* and its successor, *Take Hart*, were ostensibly programmes about art, many viewers tuned in to watch Aardman's creations. Morph was soon joined by his nemesis, Chas, and was eventually allowed his own programme, *The Amazing Adventures of Morph*, in which he gained an entire family, including Gillespie and Foily (so named because she was made out of foil).

What was remarkable about Morph was the amount of characterization that Aardman were able to achieve with their animation. The character was extremely crude – his face was just eyes and a mouth – and he spoke in gibberish, but Aardman managed to give him a vivid personality. David Sproxton says of Morph, 'That's really where Peter learned his skills, in terms of body language and expression. Because they're perfect little characters. Very, very simple.' If Morph taught them the art of characterization, it was further refined in their next projects.

Conversation Pieces

Aardman were introduced to the idea of using 'real-life' soundtracks by Bill Mather, head of graphics at the BBC, who was interested in producing a series of animations for adults. He had already done a pilot featuring his son going to a choir audition, called *Audition*, when he contacted Sproxton and Lord and commissioned them to make two films. Aardman's first films using the technique which was to become their hallmark were *Down and Out*, set in a Salvation Army hostel, and *Confessions of a Foyer Girl*, in 1978. As they made the films, they realized that these real-life soundtracks provided them with the perfect way of achieving spontaneity in animation.

The newly appointed head of Channel Four, Jeremy Isaacs, saw *Down and Out* and was impressed. Channel Four was a new television company with a remit to produce unconven-

Creature Comforts, Jaguar

tional programmes and Isaacs was keen to promote animation. Initially, he asked Aardman for ten short films for the first week of broadcast which would use the same conversational style as *Down and Out*. Aardman talked him down to five – at the time, Sproxton and Lord were still the only employees and had to do everything themselves – and then began work. The films were eventually shown in the week of Channel Four's first anniversary to great critical acclaim.

In 1989, Channel Four broadcast a further series of Aardman films under the title Lip Synch. Peter Lord directed two of this new series, *Going Equipped* and *War Story*, so as to give other animators an opportunity to make films. The interviews for *War Story* – in total, two and a half hours' worth, from which Lord selected passages to animate – were conducted by Peter Lawrence of BBC Radio Bristol. Aardman

Wat' s Pig

tried not to meet the subjects of their films before their work was completed in order to leave themselves free to come up with their own characters, but when they eventually met Bill Perry, the star of *War Story*, they were amused to see that he bore an amazing resemblance to their creation.

The Lip Synch series included the film that was to win the studio its first Oscar, Nick Park's *Creature Comforts*. Park chose to conduct the interviews himself, asking questions that would prompt answers suitable to a zoo creature. The Brazilian student immortalized as a caged jaguar was especially obliging, as he complained about the food in his halls of residence. Other animators took a different approach, Barry Purves's *Next* and Richard Goleszowski's *Ident*, for example, using minimal dialogue and preferring sound effects or simply silence.

Commercials and Music Videos

The Conversation Pieces series for Channel Four was extremely successful, resulting in awards and critical acclaim. It also led the studio to branch out in a new direction: commercials. This was an area they had never considered before, but in the mid-1980s advertising agencies were on a roll, producing more and more innovative and quirky ideas. Aardman fitted the bill. According to Sproxton, they went into it expecting a brief interlude between television projects: 'We thought animated commercials would be a brief fashion but there has proved to be a continuing demand and, basically, it's funded the studio.'

Their first project was for the Enterprise computer (in which – perhaps unwisely with hindsight – Enterprise's competitors were shown to be creaky fossils) and, armed with a much bigger budget than they were accustomed to, Aardman did their first work on 35mm film. Further commercials followed in the UK, including the famous Scotch Video skeleton (a tip of the hat towards Ray Harryhausen's stunning work on *Jason and the Argonauts*), and subsequently Aardman have produced commercials for; American Express, Cadbury's, Chewits, Duracell, Guinness, Lego, London Zoo, Polo, Smarties, Wagon Wheels and Weetabix.

The commercials produced by Aardman are wildly popular. The Heat Electric commercials inspired by *Creature Comforts* were recently voted number four in a poll to find the best UK adverts of all time and the mischievous little man who advertises Lurpack Butter (subsequently named Douglas and surely a direct descendant of Morph) is a cult icon.

The adverts benefited Aardman enormously. Financially, they enabled the company to expand, move to new premises and take on new animators, including Barry Purves (who has since left to found his own studio), Richard Goleszowski, Steve Box, Peter Peake and a young chap fresh out of film school called Nick Park. The practical experience that the commercials gave provided a further opportunity to hone the skills of the animators still further. A knock-on effect has been to give their distinctive style far greater exposure than most animators are used to, gaining a legion of fans who might not normally watch animation: the Lip Synch series was broadcast on Channel Four but the adverts for Lurpack went out to a mass audience.

In addition to their commercial work, Aardman have also been responsible for some acclaimed music videos. Their first, made in 1986, was the seminal video for Peter Gabriel's 'Sledgehammer'. Peter Lord, Richard Goleszowski and Nick Park worked with the Brothers Quay and David Anderson. It went on to win nine MTV awards (including Best Video of the Year). In addition, it won a Brit Award for Best Video and is regularly included in 'best of all time' lists. More recently, Steve Box directed the video for the Spice Girl's 'Viva Forever', which featured the Girls as animated fairies.

Lord and Sproxton decided early on to plough any profits they made back into the company. The money they have made from their work on commercials and music videos has allowed the studio to prosper and allowed them to work on more personal, less lucrative projects. Advertisers flock to their Bristol base to make use of their skills and experience, and the result is some of the finest commercials seen on television anywhere.

Heat Electric, Pigs

Nick Park

Aardman was started by David Sproxton and Peter Lord and between them they managed to turn the studio into a world-class operation, producing innovative and exciting work. However, with the arrival of Nick Park and his creations, Aardman would rise to another level.

It is fitting that Nick Park should work for Aardman since he was influenced by the animations that Sproxton and Lord produced for Vision On. In particular, Morph fired the young man's imaginations and he began to work in Plasticine, creating his own short films in the attic of his parents' house. He was trained at the prestigious National Film and Television School, where he began work on his graduation feature, *A Grand Day Out*. The school had a small budget to invite day lecturers and at Park's request they asked Sproxton and Lord along.

Nick Park showed Peter Lord the storyboards and some of his preliminary work on *A Grand Day Out* and was flattered when Lord told him that he had a good sense of direction. Park was offered work at the Aardman studios in Bristol for a month during his summer vacation (he stayed with Peter Lord and his family) and was subsequently asked to join permanently. The extra work generated by their TV commercials meant that Aardman could afford to expand for the first time.

Aardman were then working for writer/producer David Hopkins on a very ambitious fifteen-minute anti-war film called *Babylon* and they recruited Park to assist with the animation. They tempted him with the promise of resources to finish *A Grand Day Out*. After *Babylon* was completed, Park returned to his own film and, with the assistance of his new employers, managed to finish it very quickly. Peter Lord realized Park's enormous talent early on and takes enormous pride in the achievements of his protégé: 'I don't take any

Heat Electric, Frank

credit for his talent – he came to us fully fledged – but I do take credit for giving him the environment in which to make it happen.'

A Grand Day Out marked the debut of the soon to be world famous Wallace and Gromit, the jug-eared, cheese-loving inventor and his trusty canine sidekick. After their first adventure (a trip to the moon to find cheese), Nick Park put them aside to work on other projects, including *Creature Comforts* for the Lip Synch series. As mentioned before, this was the first Aardman film to win an Oscar (for Best Animated Short Film in 1991) and inspired the incredibly popular Heat Electric advertising campaign.

The success of Creature Comforts meant that work could

begin on Wallace and Gromit's next adventure. Park has said that he based Wallace on his father, an inveterate inventor of gadgets, which explains all the Heath-Robinson apparatus that clutters up Wallace's house. Unlike *A Grand Day Out*, where Park had to do everything by himself, the new film had a full crew and Bob Baker assisted in the writing. *The Wrong Trousers* (named after the ex-NASA 'techno-trousers' hijacked by a villainous penguin) was co-financed by the BBC and shown to high ratings over the Christmas period. It demonstrates just how far Park had developed as a film makerr. The film has much higher production values, picked up from Aardman's work on commercials, and shows an even greater control of the material. Unsurprisingly, it was rewarded with another Oscar and spawned an eventual £50 million worth of merchandising.

The trilogy was completed with *A Close Shave*, an everyday story of window-cleaning, sheep rustling and cyber-dogs. Again, the BBC showed this at Christmas to a huge and appreciative audience and once more Park picked up an Oscar (he has won more Oscars than any other living person). In 1997, he was awarded the CBE.

Following the success of *Chicken Run*, which he co-directed with Peter Lord, Nick Park has begun work on the inevitable – and much anticipated – Wallace and Gromit feature film. For the moment, however, the plot is under close wraps.

Other Projects

The success of Nick Park has never inhibited the other work that goes on at Aardman. In addition to Wallace and Gromit, the studio produces a variety of other characters, including Rex the Runt, created and directed by Richard Goleszowski.

Rex began life as part of Goleszowski's Lip Synch film, *Ident*, and over a period of seven years the character was refined and developed, involving the production of no fewer than three pilot episodes (*Dinosaurs*, *Dreams* and *North by North Pole*). These early adventures have been memorably described by an admirer as 'some of the most surreal in Plasticine dog history'. In 1998, Rex began a series of thirteen adventures on BBC2, with the promise of more to come.

Aardman's latest creation was devised exclusively for the Internet. Angry Kid, a carrot-topped juvenile troublemaker, has his one-minute escapades broadcast on-line by Atom Films. He was created by Darren Walsh, who also directs and provides the voices. David Sproxton was keen to use the Internet: 'We believe the Internet could very well prove to be one of the most exciting platforms for entertainment distribution.' The Kid's adventures have certainly proved popular: they passed 1 million downloads in just seven weeks on-line.

Hollywood studios had been courting Aardman for some time, wanting them to produce a full-length feature film, but Aardman rejected them until they considered themselves

Humdrum

ready. When the time was right, they signed a five-picture deal with Dreamworks SKG, the progressive new studio established by Steven Spielberg and Jeffrey Katzenberg. Katzenberg was responsible for saving Disney Studios in the 1980s and has always considered animation to be a top priority. It was natural, therefore, that he should turn to Aardman. After many nights burning the midnight oil, the first film in the deal was released in 2000. *Chicken Run* ('a prisoner of war escape movie but with chickens,' as Peter Lord describes it) was directed by Peter Lord and Nick Park. It has grossed over $100 million at US box offices alone.

Aardman's immediate slate includes work on their second feature film, an updated version of 'The Hare and the Tortoise', which is due to be released in 2002. It is being directed by Richard Goleszowski and will feature the vocal talents of Sir Michael Caine.

The Future

Aardman is a successful company with a consistent track record that has attracted a solid fan base. However, the stop-motion approach is coming increasingly under threat from computers. Indeed, Hollywood (the greatest patron of stop motion) has abandoned all forms of traditional stop motion in favour of computer technology, which has proliferated since it was used so successfully on Steven Spielberg's *Jurassic Park*. The incredible success of *Toy Story* (directed by John Lasseter, a good friend to Aardman) has shown that traditional cel animation is also under siege.

Aardman has always embraced technology that would enhance the quality of their work, especially the performance aspect, but have never lost sight of the fundamental principles behind character animation.

'The principles of good animation are the same for whatever medium – body language, gravity, balance, expression

Wat's Pig

and acting. Given a reasonable understanding of those, the technique is then very much more one of performance with clay, as opposed to the conventional approach of keys, in-betweening and extrapolation with computers,' states David Sproxton. Computers, it should be remembered, are a tool and as such are only as good as the people using them.

Aardman are now the most respected model animators in the world. By using their profits to build up the studio, David Sproxton and Peter Lord have been able to train many young animators. *Chicken Run* has introduced a new age group to stop-motion animation. It is true to say that Sproxton and Lord have influenced a generation, just as Ray Harryhausen influenced them.

They have come a long way from the kitchen-table experiments, to the point where serious comparisons can be made with Disney's animation studios. They have an instantly recognizable house style and a menagerie of beloved characters. Wallace and Gromit adorn nearly as many T-shirts as Mickey and Donald, with more characters poised to emulate their success. There's no Aardworld planned yet, but maybe in the future fans will be able to ride to the moon with Wallace and Gromit or have their own (mis)adventures with Angry Kid. But until then, they'll just have to be content with watching the animations again – and take comfort from the fact that Aardman are busy producing more work for them to enjoy.

An Introduction to Animation

Aardman are now as influential as their idol Ray Harryhausen and are just as instrumental in encouraging many young people to take up animation. After watching the films you might want to try animation yourself. But be warned: you need perseverance and dedication to become a good animator. You'll have to develop your natural talents over a period of years, learning from the many mistakes that, sadly, are inevitable. If that hasn't deterred you, then please read on.

What follows is only a very basic guide to animation. The best and most comprehensive book to read is Aardman's own *Cracking Animation* by Peter Lord and Brian Sibley. It's full of excellent advice for the novice animator and is the best way of studying the Aardman style.

Getting Started

People were making animations even before the camera was invented. The basic principle of animation is to put together a series of pictures that move fast enough to fool the eye into thinking that continuous activity is taking place. The simplest form of animation is the flick book, where there is a drawing on the first page, a slight variant of that drawing on the next page and so on. By quickly flicking through the pages, the illusion of movement is created.

In order to make stop-motion animations you'll need a camera. Although many people have domestic camcorders, these aren't particularly useful for animation, even if they promise animation facilities. They can only take around a quarter of a second per shot, which means that any image will be much jerkier than it would be if you were using a cine camera. It's possible to use a computer to store images collected on a video camera and then animate them in the computer, but again this offers much less flexibility than film.

Pib & Pog

However, if you have access to a video camera that offers animation facilities, it's not a bad place to start, as video technology is advancing rapidly. It's technically easier to shoot on 35 mm film but finding processing facilities is getting harder and harder.

First Steps

OK, so now you're armed with your camera and you're ready to begin animating. But don't start work on your feature film just yet; like everything else, you have to learn to walk before you can run.

The more ambitious the animation is, the more preparation you'll need to do first. For a beginner, it's best to start with an easy idea so that you can begin to get practical experience straight away. As we've already seen, Peter Lord and David Sproxton started their animation career with a simple figure drawn on a blackboard, so if you've got some chalk to hand you could easily follow their lead. Alternatively, why not start by animating simple household objects? Take an angle-poise lamp or maybe a computer mouse as your model. Although it uses computer animation, John Lasseter's *Luxo Jr* – a short film about two lamps playing with a rubber ball – shows how much character inanimate objects can be given by an imaginative animator.

Story

Of course, to make a successful animation you need to have your subjects doing something. In other words, you need a story. For animation, a story doesn't have to be very compli-cated – indeed, at the beginning it might be limited simply to having a computer mouse swarm over a table – but you must know what you're going to do.

Once you've planned an idea, you should begin to develop it in more detail. Work out what you want to happen in your story. Don't be too ambitious at this stage. Until you've mastered the basic techniques, try to keep your ideas as simple as possible.

The next step is to prepare a storyboard. As the name sug-gests, a storyboard is a breakdown of the story in graphic form, with illustrations to demonstrate every action in the film like a comic strip. You should aim to make your storyboard as detailed as possible, since it will be your guide while making your animation. It doesn't matter if you're not very good at drawing as you can just use stick figures. The important thing is that all the information you need is clearly laid out so that you can see what you're doing.

Location

Aardman began on David Sproxton's kitchen table. In other words, you don't need a special studio to do animations – you can do them anywhere. However, there are a few things you must to bear in mind. You'll need somewhere with a firm base that won't wobble all over the place, so rickety tables and soft furnishings are a bad idea. Equally, you'll be busy for a long period of time, so don't set up shop where you're likely to be disturbed or you'll inconvenience people.

Models

When you first start to build models, go for simple figures so that you don't cause yourself too many problems. Model making is a skill in itself and you'll need to develop your abilities, so when you're starting out simplicity is the best approach. Morph was an extremely simple figure but was successful because of the animation.

The best material to use is Plasticine. It's cheap, readily available and easy to manipulate. Roll it around in your hands to warm it up and away you go. The easiest shape to make is a worm, which can be modelled quickly and is easy to animate. When building more complicated figures, you need to take account of things like gravity – it's no use having a character whose head is twice the size of its body since it will just fall over. Remember that these models are going to be moved about, so make sure they are sturdy enough to withstand days of filming.

Animating!

Without doubt, the best way to learn animation is by experience so that you learn from your mistakes. There are very few rules in animation – you just have to find out what works for you.

The really important thing to remember is that nothing should move unless you want it to. Because animation is shot frame by frame, any disturbance will destroy the film, so you have to keep the camera steady (a tripod is the best method) and make sure that none of the models wobble. Take care when repositioning your figures to preserve the continuity

Pib & Pog

and don't knock them. Be careful with the backgrounds as well – everything must be firmly locked in place so that it doesn't get moved. Remember, if you are concentrating on the main characters you might not notice that the background has shifted, but your audience certainly will.

It's up to you to determine how characters move, but the most successful animations often aim to create a naturalistic approach, with the characters moving like real people no matter how outlandish their appearance. Even the most bizarre of Aardman's characters behave in a naturalistic way, which is one of the reasons why people respond to their work. The best way to achieve this is to 'act out' your characters' movements beforehand and then coax your models into copying you. Fortunately, you'll be on your own, so there won't be anyone to see you pulling unusual faces or pretending to be a strange creature.

A Few Last Things...

As we've stressed again and again, the most important thing is to practise and to keep working at things. It will take time to get to a reasonable standard, but along the way you'll learn much that will help you.

Although you should aim for simplicity at the beginning, you'll soon progress and become more adventurous, building better figures and creating more imaginative sets. The *Cracking Animations* book is an excellent starting-point, but don't limit yourself – experiment. Try new techniques and, if you have an idea, go with it. Remember, you have nothing to lose and the only constraint is your imagination. The most important thing to keep telling yourself is that this should be *fun*.

Heat Electric, Penguins

Creature Comforts, Polar Bears

Heat Electric, Pablo

Creature Comforts, Bluebird

Creature Comforts, Terrapins

Heat Electric, Pigs

Minotaur and Little Nerkins

Al Dente

Owzat

Pib & Pog

Humdrum

Wat's Pig

Creature Comforts, Rodents
right *Heat Electeric, Carol and Dog, Penguins*

Heat Electric, Frank

Selected Filmography

Feature Films

2000
Chicken Run
Direction: Nick Park and Peter Lord

Short Films

1978
ANIMATED CONVERSATIONS
Confessions of a Foyer Girl and *Down and Out*
Direction/Animation: Peter Lord and David Sproxton
5 minutes each

1981–3
The Amazing Adventures of Morph (26 episodes)
Direction/Animation: Peter Lord and David Sproxton
5 minutes each

CONVERSATION PIECES
On Probation, *Sales Pitch*, *Palmy Days*, *Early Bird* and *Late Edition*
Direction/Animation: Peter Lord and David Sproxton
5 minutes each

1986
Babylon
Direction/Animation: Peter Lord and David Sproxton
14 minutes 30 seconds

1989
LIP SYNCH
Next
Direction/Animation: Barry Purves
Ident
Direction/Animation: Richard Goleszowski
Going Equipped
Direction/Animation: Peter Lord
Creature Comforts
Direction/Animation: Nick Park

War Story
Direction/Animation: Peter Lord
5 minutes each

A Grand Day Out
Direction/Animation: Nick Park
23 minutes
(production: the National Film and Television School and finished with the help of Aardman Animations)

Lifting the Blues
Direction/Animation: David Sproxton
52 minutes

1991
Rex the Runt – How Dinosaurs Became Extinct
Direction/Animation: Richard Goleszowski
2 minutes

Rex the Runt – Dreams
Direction/Animation: Richard Goleszowski
2 minutes

Adam
Direction/Animation: Peter Lord
6 minutes

1992
Never Say Pink Furry Die
Direction/Animation: Louise Spraggon
12 minutes

Loves Me, Loves Me Not
Direction/Animation: Jeff Newitt
8 minutes

1993
The Wrong Trousers
Direction: Nick Park
Animation: Nick Park and Steve Box
29 minutes

Not Without My Handbag
Direction/Animation: Boris Kossmehl
12 minutes

1994
Pib and Pog
Direction/Animation: Peter Peake
6 minutes

1995
A Close Shave
Direction: Nick Park
Animation: Nick Park, Steve Box, Peter Peake, Loyd Price,
Gary Cureton, Ian Whitlock and Sergio Delfino
29 minutes

1996
Pop
Direction/Animation: Sam Fell
5 minutes
Wat's Pig
Direction: Peter Lord
Animation: Peter Lord, Sam Fell and Mike Booth
11 minutes

Rex the Runt – North by North Pole
Direction: Richard Goleszowski
Animation: Richard Goleszowski, Chris Sadler, Dave Osmond, Sergio Delfino and Grant White
6 minutes

1997
Stage Fright
Direction: Steve Box
Animation: Jason Spencer-Galsworthy, Gary Cureton, Loyd Price and Dave Osmond
11 minutes

Owzat
Direction/Animation: Mark Brierly
5 minutes

Rex the Runt (13 episodes)
Direction: Richard Goleszowski
Animation: Various

1998
Hum Drum
Direction/Animation: Peter Peake
6 minutes

Al Dente
Direction/Animation: Mark Brierly
2 minutes
Angry Kid (3 episodes)
Direction/Animation: Darren Walsh

1999
Minotaur and Little Nerkin
Direction/Animation: Nick Mackie
Angry Kid (13 episodes)
Direction/Animation: Darren Walsh

Rabbits!
Direction/Animation: Sam Fell

Music Videos

1986
'Sledgehammer'
Direction: Stephen Johnson
Animation: Peter Lord, Nick Park, Richard Goleszowski and
the Brothers Quay
4 minutes 30 seconds

1987
'Barefootin''
Direction/Animation: Richard Goleszowski
2 minutes 30 seconds

'My Baby Just Cares for Me'
Direction/Animation: Peter Lord
3 minutes

1988
'Harvest for the World'
Direction/Animation (animation sequence only): David
Sproxton, Peter Lord and Richard Goleszowski
4 minutes

1996
'Never in Your Wildest Dreams'
Direction: Bill Mather
Animation: Paul Smith, Olly Reid and Sergio Delfino
4 minutes

'Viva Forever'
Direction: Steve Box
Animation: Steve Box and Darren Robbie
5 minutes

Television Sequences

Victoria Wood (BBC)
Heart of the Country (BBC)

1986
Pee-Wee Herman Show – Penny
Direction/Animation: David Sproxton, Peter Lord, Nick Park
and Richard Goleszowski

1987
Spitting Image
Animation: Peter Lord, Nick Park, Richard Goleszowski and
Dave Alex Riddett

1988
Comic Relief
Direction: David Sproxton
Animation: Fred Reed

Amnesty International Concert for Human Rights
Direction: Stephen Johnson
Animation: Richard Goleszowski and Andy Staveley

Friday Night Live
Direction/Animation: Nick Park

1999
Comic Relief
Direction/Animation: Richard Goleszowski

SELECTED AWARDS

Nick Park
Royal Television Society, UK, 1992, Sir Ambrose Fleming
Award

Los Angeles Film Critics' Association, USA, 1996, Best
Animation 'For His Body of Work'

David Sproxton
Rassengradi Palermon International Sports Film Festival, Italy,
1989, Diploma

A Close Shave

British Animation Awards, UK, 1996: Best Film over Fifteen
Minutes, Best Scenario, Public Choice Award for Favourite
Film, Public Choice Award for Funniest Film

Academy of Motion Picture Arts and Sciences, USA, 1996 Best
Animated Short Film (Oscar®)

BAFTA, 1995, Best Animated Film

The Chicago International Children's Film Festival, USA, 1996,
Outstanding Director Award

Best Animated Short, European Licensing Awards, 1996,
Character Property of The Year

Goldfish, Russia, 1996, Special Prize for Character

First Prize World Animation Celebration, 1997, First Prize, Best
Animation

International Emmy Awards, USA, 1996, Best Popular Arts
Programme

Royal Television Society Craft and Design Awards, UK, 1996,
Best Production Design, Best Sound, Judges' Award

A Grand Day Out

BAFTA, UK, 1990, Best Short Animated Film

British Animation Awards, UK, 1990, Best Film over Fifteen
Minutes

Academy of Motion Picture Arts and Sciences, Nomination for
Best Short Animated Film

Adam

BAFTA, 1992, Nomination

28th Chicago International Film Festival, 1992, Silver Plaque

Shanghai International Film Festival, China, 1992, First Prize,
Category B (5–15 Minutes)

Academy of Motion Picture Arts and Sciences, USA, 1992,
Nomination for Best Animated Short Film

Amazing Adventures of Morph

BAFTA, 1980, Nomination

Creature Comforts

Academy of Motion Picture Arts and Sciences, USA, 1990,
Best Short Animated Film (Oscar®)

British Animation Awards, UK, 1990, Best Film under Fifteen
Minutes

Annecy, France, 1991, Special Jury Prize, Best Use of Humour

Belgium, 1991, Golden Cartoon

Melbourne International Film Festival, Australia, 1991, Most
Popular Short Film

UNICEF honorary diploma

Down and Out

Melbourne International Film Festival, Australia, 1981,
Animation Award

Hum Drum
Edinburgh Film Festival, Scotland, 1998, Post Office Mclaren
    Award for Best Animated Film
BAFTA, 1999, Nomination for Best Short Animated Film
British Animation Awards, 2000, Best Film, Public Choice
    Award
Mons, Belgium, 1999, Golden Monkey for Best Animation
Chicago International Children's Film Festival, 1999, FirstPrize
New York International Children's Film Festival, 1999, Grand
    Prize
Napoli Film Festival, Italy, 1999, Short Volcano Award
Hiroshima Film Festival, Japan, 2000, Special Jury Prize

Loves Me Loves Me Not
Chicago International Film Festival, 1992, Certificate of Merit

Minotaur and Little Nerkin
Synthesis Festival, Belgium, 2000, Best Humour in a Short
    Film

My Baby Just Cares For Me
Cannes, France, 1988, Diploma

Not Without My Handbag
Tampere Film festival, Finland, 1994, Best International
    Animation
Dresden International Film Festival, Germany, 1994, Joint First
    Prize for Animation
Braunschweig, Germany, 1994, Audience Prize

Pib and Pog
BAFTA, 1994, Nomination
Edinburgh Film Festival, Scotland, 1995, Post Office Mclaren
    Award

The Everyman Cinema Award for Best Animation over Five
Minutes, 1995

POP
Ziln Festival, Czech Republic May, 1997, Children's Jury Prize
for Best Animated Film

Rex the Runt
The Indies, London, 2000, Carlton Award for International
Animation

Stage Fright
BAFTA, 1998, Best Short Animated Film
Annecy, France, 1998, Children's Jury Prize
Dong-a-Ling, Korea May, 1998, First Prize
Jerusalem International Film Festival, 1998, Best International
Animation

The Wrong Trousers
38th Cork Film Festival, Ireland, 1993, Special Jury
Commendation
Academy of Motion Picture Arts and Sciences, 1994, Best
Short Animated Film (Oscar®)
BAFTA, UK, 1994, Best Short Animated Film
Seattle International Film Festival, USA, 1994, Golden Space
Needle Award for Best Short Film
Sydney Film Festival, Australia, 1994, Audience Prize for Best
Short Film
Film Critics Circle Prize for Best Short Film, Blackpool Film
Festival, England, 1994, Golden Tower Award
European Association of Animated Film, Belgium, 1994,
Golden Cartoon
Krok Animation Festival, Ukraine, 1995, Special Jury Prize

War Story
BAFTA, UK, 1990, Nomination

Wat's Pig
Academy of Motion Picture Arts and Sciences, USA, 1996,
    Nomination for Best Short Film
New York Film Festival, 1996, Silver Medal for Short Film
    (Animated)

In addition, Aardman have won numerous awards for their
advertisements and for their work on music videos. In total,
they have been awarded 234 awards from organizations and
film festivals across the world.

Resources

Books

For anyone interested in learning more about Aardman, the best book is Aardman's own *Cracking Animation* by Peter Lord and Brian Sibley. It offers a history of the studio and a comprehensive guide to the processes involved in creating an animation.

Also of interest is Brian Sibley's book *'Chicken Run' Hatching the Movie*, a detailed inside look at the production of Aardman's first feature film.

The Internet

Surfers in search of the ultimate Aardman experience are advised to point their browser towards the official Aardman website (www.Aardman.com), which contains a full listing for every project. All the official sites for their characters can be accessed through the site and there's also an online shop that sells Aardman merchandise.

Angry Kid's adventures can be downloaded from the Atom Films website (www.atomfilms.com).

Nick Park has his own dedicated Usenet newsgroup (alt.animation.nick-park), where fans can discuss his work.